Four Truths

Four Truths

STEVEN SCHROEDER

WIPF & STOCK · Eugene, Oregon

FOUR TRUTHS
Steven Schroeder

Interior and cover images © Debby Sou Vai Keng. Used with
permission

Wipf & Stock
An Imprint of Wipf and Stock Publishers
199 W. 8th Ave., Suite 3
Eugene, OR 97401

www.wipfandstock.com

ISBN 13: 978-1-61097-449-3

Manufactured in the U.S.A.

Contents

Acknowledgments

Special thanks to Debby Sou Vai Keng for the beautiful paintings she did especially for this book. Readers interested in her work can find more at http://vacpoetry.org/debbysouvaikeng.

"Job's Cat" first appeared in *Mother of Invention*, 1999.

An earlier version of "Why Sarah Laughed" first appeared in *Rambunctious Review*, Volume XI, 1994-1995.

ONE

Job's Cat

The two were old friends.

I noticed them one day on the road in front of J's house and knew from the start that neither could be trusted.

One was a vagabond who hadn't bathed in weeks. His hair was matted. A moustache perched perilously on his upper lip like a twisted caterpillar in slow painful transit to his chin, leaving his mouth mostly hidden. His beard was a staging area for remnants of his last meal and an archaeological site in which others were preserved at varying depths. Bad grooming is one thing, but this character was jerky, bird-like, and that rubbed me the wrong way. His head bobbed. He had raptor eyes, like high flying birds that take in everything at once—impossibly intelligent and cold at the same time. He looked right through you but didn't focus: now here, now there, first one thing, then another.

The other was slick, fashionably dressed, not a thread or a hair out of place. I wondered how he could stand on that dusty road without showing a speck of dust. Maybe that's why the two hung together: Bird was a magnet for dust who kept Slick spotless.

"What have you been up to now?" Bird says.

"With you every separation is nothing but a breath in the middle of an endless conversation," says Slick.

"Well?"

"It's been years. You might begin with 'Hello. It's been a long time, and I missed you. How have you been?'"

"Hello. What have you been up to now?"

"Wandering here and there. Trying to keep things under control."

"Have you?"

"More or less. At least I attend to one thing at a time."

"There's your problem. You must have noticed J; isn't he a trip? The man dreams up rituals that wouldn't come to me in a thousand years—thinks they keep him prosperous and his children safe. Some are really entertaining. Have you seen him? He's unshakable."

"Not unshakable, just unshaken."

"Come again?"

"No reason to doubt. Let him lose some possessions, and I promise he'll be shaken."

"Promise?"

"Without a doubt."

"No doubt. That calls for a test."

I slipped under the hedge and lost sight of the two for an instant. When I looked back, Slick was alone, watching J's house. A messenger, out of breath, dashed in through the gate and pounded on the door. Lucky I'd moved, or he would have stepped on my tail. The door opened, and I saw J.

"Yes?" he said.

"I have terrible news," said the breathless messenger. "There's been a riot. Looters sacked your store and killed the entire staff. I am left alone to tell the tale."

Before he was finished, another messenger showed up and said, "What was left of the store was struck by lightning and burned down. The fire spread to your warehouse facility, and it was a total loss. Nothing is salvageable. I am left alone to tell the tale."

A third messenger showed up. I made sure I was completely out of sight.

"There's been a carjacking. The Mercedes. The chauffeur murdered," he said. "The BMW was parked at the warehouse and exploded when the fire spread. I am left alone to tell the tale."

At that moment, a small, serious looking man with a briefcase showed up: J's accountant. "Bad news, J. Somebody failed to make your insurance payments, and the policy's lapsed. None of your losses are covered."

Another messenger arrived, sobbing: "Your children and their families were all together at your oldest son's house when a tornado struck. The roof collapsed, and they were all killed. I am left alone to tell the tale."

What else could go wrong? I lay *real* low.

J said a little prayer, and I saw Slick smile. Then he was not there.

I was considering going into the house for a bite to eat when I heard them on the other side of the hedge.

"Well," said Bird. "What have you been up to now?"

"Wandering here and there. Trying to keep things under control."

"Have you?"

"More or less. At least I attend to one thing at a time."

Like nothing happened.

"You must have noticed J. Just unshakable."

"Not unshakable, just unshaken."

"Come again?"

"Let him suffer pain, and I promise he'll be shaken."

"Promise?"

"Without a doubt."

"No doubt. That calls for a test."

Bird was gone. Slick kept watching.

J came out onto the porch. He was scratching, like he had hives or something. I thought of fleas again, and rolled in the dust under the hedge. But I made sure Slick didn't see me there. J was covered with nasty sores.

Now M, who lived with us in the house, joined J on the porch.

"You *are* a mess," she said. "What have you gotten yourself in to?"

"Nothing," J said. "It has nothing to do with anything I've done."

M was not convinced. She went inside.

Slick smiled.

Then company came.

A bunch of J's friends heard about his problems and came to call. At first, they all just sat on the porch. They said nothing. They sat there for a week.

Slick was there the whole time, but Bird was nowhere.

Then J complained.

"These damn sores hurt so much I'd rather be dead. What the hell is going on?"

One of J's friends jumped in as if cued: "You know, J, you must have done something that could explain all this."

"I've done nothing. And what could I possibly have done that would explain any of this? I'm sick, ready to die; but I've done nothing to deserve it."

Another friend said, "You know, J, the world's a reasonable place, and God's in charge. Why don't we get down on our knees right here right now and take it to the Lord in prayer?"

Like Bird said, J was a trip. You'd think he'd go for an impromptu ritual—but he asked for an attorney!

"God is my tormenter," he said. "And I want to sue. All I need is a high enough court and a good enough litigator."

He was joking. Or delusional.

Slick got it. He smiled. I thought for a moment he was going to step forward. Chances are he *is* an attorney. He looked the part. And he looked ready to take the case.

But another friend piped in: "Come on, J. You know nobody's perfect. No need to take God to court; just own whatever you've done and ask God to make things right."

Slick hung back. I lay low.

J went off. A *long* speech about God being in charge and therefore responsible for bad as well as good.

Now Slick looked like an attorney who expected a substantial out of court settlement—plenty of profit, no trial. He kept smiling.

J and his friends went at it again. The gist of it was that the friends thought it had to make sense while J insisted that it didn't but should. He wanted nothing but his day in court.

By this time, I was tired and hungry—how long had we been at this?—and I was starting to have trouble following the discussion. But I couldn't leave. I had to see how things would turn out, and I didn't want Slick or Bird to spot me. I was amazed at Slick's single-minded concentration. Bird was all over the place, long ago off to other things; but Slick's attention never wavered. He was right there, attending to one thing alone.

J was thoroughly ticked off with his reasonable friends. He wanted nothing but a hearing. He was miserable, and he thought he was entitled to shout about it. Too bad he wasn't aware of Slick there, just listening.

Then another friend showed up, a young guy, excitable. He wanted to preach. J wanted to smack him, but they all let him proceed with a homily on God's inscrutability.

Then Bird showed up out of nowhere with his cold raptor eyes. Nobody knew *where* he came from, but they'd been at this so long and they were so tired and hungry that hallucinations went without saying. They weren't surprised, and they let him rant. He went on about taking everything in at once and stared them down one by one with his cold superior raptor eyes.

I thought Slick would laugh out loud.

J had nothing to say.

Bird told J's friends off, looked around, and was gone.

More friends showed up, each with a load of gifts. J was rich again.

Like nothing happened.

Turns out M had left long ago, and I decided to go find her. J had nothing to say, and M would feed me.

Bird was gone. Slick was smiling. Bird would come again, and the interval for him would be a breath in a long conversation with his only friend.

I miss the kids and M. The chauffeur gave me tuna. The Beemer had soft seats. The Mercedes engine well was a warm place to sleep outside in winter.

The two are old friends. Neither can be trusted.

I am left alone to tell the tale.

one: dukha

1. In "the West," where Greek thinking took root in Judaism and its offspring, Christianity and Islam, the *fact* of suffering has given rise to a rich tradition of theodicy. Affirming God's power and God's goodness together demands *reason* of suffering. Suffering without reason poses a problem for God, for faith, or for both.

2. Reason has clustered as much around control and knowledge as around power and goodness, and theodicies have often been embodied in languages of limits. That human beings cannot make sense of suffering has been attributed to the fact that human intellect is limited: suffering's senselessness is a result of the partial perspective of finite beings. From a God's-eye view, the senselessness of suffering is absorbed into the sense of the whole. God's limitlessness limits suffering—making it disappear at the limit, passing in time or, through some whole seen, passing into something else.

3. As a language of limits, theodicy turns on finitude and time and is as concerned with sense as with suffering. Suffering that does not pass is punishment: it is incontrovertible evidence that something intrinsic to the sufferer is suffering's cause. At the limit,

there is no *innocent* suffering, because there can be no suffering without cause.

4. Which makes theodicy, more often than not, a search for some *other* to blame.

5. In Islam, which is most adamant in its affirmation of God's power, theodicy simply vanishes into reason: there can be no innocent suffering, because God cannot be in any way associated with evil. The problem, then, is not accounting for innocent suffering but rather discovering why it is not innocent. Suffering must be put on trial and the sufferer convicted. Christianity has sometimes taken a similar turn, but it has also admitted an instance of innocent suffering made necessary (and thus explained) by sin. Judaism has often turned on time and embraced patience, confident enough of the end to wait suffering out.

6. Common to "Western" accounts of suffering is confidence that it dissolves in the power and goodness of God—whether gradually, across time, or all at once, because God's power is present and absolute in every instant. But what is perhaps less obvious is that this places knowledge against a background of suffering. Because God's knowledge is not limited, it recognizes that suffering is nothing in itself, only part of a whole that is good. Bearing suffering with patience (submission, as Islam puts it) leads to *knowledge* that is more like the whole knowledge of God—or subjects us to that knowledge itself. This is not so different from the Greek understanding

of passion developed at length in the tradition of tragic drama: what we suffer becomes our teacher, and it is not reality but our vision that changes in the process. Our eyes change in time, so, though nothing changes, time changes everything.

7.   But this confidence in vision poses problems, particularly when one claims to see with God's eyes—waiting in the expectation of an end (now or then) in which one sees with such eyes: the expectation of an end is a narrative temptation endemic to the West. More than once, an *end* of history has been used to make mass murder make sense.

8.   In the garden, the temptation was not the fruit: we have no reason to doubt that it was good to eat. The temptation was to be like gods. And that is why a story that begins with old friends meeting like gods in the court of heaven and ends as though nothing had changed should give us pause. The two were old friends. Neither could be trusted. All that accounts for the suffering of Job is a chance encounter and a series of wagers. As if nothing would change.

9.   In the end, the tale survives in the teller alone. We know nothing but the tale in the telling and the trace of the teller.

TWO

Why Sarah Laughed

Sarah was dreaming again.

She was a little girl whose father had been away for a long time, fighting a war she didn't understand. He was coming home today, and she was beside herself with excitement. All morning, she had been watching the road, straining to catch a glimpse of him the moment he came into view. Even before she could see him, she saw the dust rising from the road, and she half danced, half ran toward his arrival.

She expected him to smile, to receive her with a laugh and an embrace. He had been away a long time.

But when his face became clear, she saw that it was distorted with anger and pain, and he shouted, "What have you done?"

"What have I done?" she thought. "And why does even my dancing out to welcome my father home cause him such pain?"

She looked at his face again, and saw that it was Abraham.

The first time Sarah told her therapist this dream, she thought she saw a hunger in his eyes, as though he thought the dream would feed him. But that was crazy, so she put it out of her mind. He encouraged her to write her dreams down, to bind them and bring them to him.

She had never talked about her dreams before, or even tried to remember them. But as soon as she spoke this one, she remembered that she had dreamed it before, and that there were many other dreams like it.

"Good, good...," said her therapist, and he told her to remember them all.

Her father, Jephthah, was a great general, and the whole country depended on him. They had forgotten him when they were at peace. But the moment they found themselves in trouble, they begged him to save them.

He laughed and said, "If I save you, you'll owe me." They knew and he knew that they would owe him their existence. He would not let them forget that again.

Jephthah went out with a mighty army, confident of victory: God was on his side. He rode back in triumph.

And when he saw his daughter dancing, he was angry.

Sarah looked at his face and saw that it was Abraham.

"What have I done?" she asked.

Jephthah told his story as one of infinite pain.

"I went out at the head of a mighty army, and I spoke to God. I promised God that, if He would deliver my enemies into my hands, I would sacrifice the first living thing I saw upon my return. I spoke to God...I promised...I bound myself...I bound God...What have you done?"

The story went on and on, and Sarah tried to listen to her father's voice. But it was indistinguishable from the moaning of the wind, and all she could hear was "I, I, I..." and "God, God, God..." She noticed that it had become suddenly cold.

"If you promised, Father..."

She woke up, shaking. She was freezing, and she couldn't breathe. She turned on the light and wrote the dream in the book she kept for her therapist. She tried to go back to sleep.

Another time, she was her father the general. She rode out on a fine horse with a mighty army, confident that she would save her people and prove that God was on her side.

When they met the enemy, she looked into his eyes, and saw that it was her child, Isaac. It was the most terrible thing she had ever seen. They were all children, and she was leading an army that was slaughtering them. She looked at her army, and again she saw Isaac. They were all children, and they were covered with blood.

"What have I done?" she said.

She rode home in shame. When she saw her daughter dancing, she saw herself, and it made her angry, because it reminded her of her pain.

She woke up, shaking. She was freezing, and she couldn't breathe. Her husband Abraham was snoring. She turned on the light and stumbled down the hall to her child's room. She watched for a long time to assure herself that Isaac was breathing regularly. She wrote the dream in the book she kept for her therapist. She tried to go back to sleep.

She heard a voice.

"Abraham," it said.

At first, she thought the voice was speaking to her husband, but then she realized that she was Abraham.

"Abraham," the voice repeated.

"What is it?" she said.

"I want you to take your child, your only child, and sacrifice him to me."

"Who are you?"

"You mustn't hesitate. The future depends on your sacrifice."

"Who are you?" she repeated.

"He has to become hard, like Abraham and Jephthah. He has to go to war. He has to learn to say 'I' as though his voice carried the authority of the north wind."

She woke up again, and walked back to Isaac's room. She looked at his face and saw that it was Abraham.

She wrote this down.

She went downstairs and sat at the kitchen table, in the dark. This was not a dream.

She remembered her life with Abraham. They had been married for over twenty years. It was the craziest thing when this child Isaac was born: she was forty years old, Abraham was forty-five, and, she thought, neither of them expected it.

She laughed.

Isaac was the child of the one moment of spontaneous passion in their entire marriage, an oversight.

Two years ago, she had discovered that Abraham was having an affair with his secretary. It seemed more like something that would have happened thirty years ago, but the man was a Neanderthal, and his secretary was caught in a time warp. When she confronted him, he blamed her. He said she had encouraged it, because *she* certainly never expressed any interest in *him* at all.

The funniest thing, though, was that she believed him.

So she "expressed interest," Abraham broke off the affair, fired his secretary, and Isaac was born.

She learned later that the "affair" had been going on for ten years, and that Isaac had an older brother.

Abraham, it seemed, was able to put this out of his mind as easily as he put "the other woman" out of his life and out of her job.

Sarah began seeing a therapist, and he told her to write down all her dreams.

She was still sitting at the kitchen table when Abraham came down for breakfast. He didn't know that she was seeing a therapist or that she would leave him as soon as she felt strong enough.

"I had the strangest dream last night," he said.

Sarah wondered when she would feel strong enough.

She laughed.

two: tanha

10.   Before he could say "it is finished," so the story goes, Jesus had to say "I thirst." By tradition, god's dying passes in seven words through suffering and thirst to forgiveness and death.

11.   The reason for forgiveness is ignorance: they do not know what they are doing.

12.   Suffering passes through thirst, even for one who does. The difference between one who does and the ones who do not lies not in thirst or in suffering but in knowing.

13.   And that, remember, was the temptation in the other story, the one this one was told to finish.

14.   To finish, write your nightmares: get dying in order by putting every single death in place. Or raise a wet sponge high enough to touch the dry lips of a thirsty god.

THREE

Oresteia: A Homecoming

The Sentinel has been watching and waiting for the return of Agamemnon and the army of Argos, who have been away at war with Troy for ten years. The Sentinel's voice at the beginning is a messianic prologue, an Advent meditation. It may be spoken or sung in a tenor or countertenor voice. Small candles (like those used in Christian churches for Easter or Christmas Eve vigils) are distributed to audience members as they enter. These small candles will be lit in a ceremony that takes place later in the play, so there should be enough "plants" in the audience to make this happen without explicit verbal instruction. There are altars at each corner of the theater. Action takes place at each of these altars, as well as at the main altar (or on stage). As the audience enters, the theater space is lit only by candles at the various altars. Before action begins, the candles are extinguished one by one in a solemn ceremony that reduces the theater/church to complete darkness, Tenebrae.

A lone voice, the Sentinel (*center, front*):
Waiting, waiting for the fire that marks an end to war,
I have surrendered to necessity and learned to read the stars.
They appear to rule the sky, mark time's march—
But their rising and their setting is fixed as my solitude;
My reading is nothing more than shared surrender;

And our companion is not sleep but fear.
Queen Clytemnestra rules in the place
Of Agamemnon's absence, her
Iron will order disordered.
But tonight, may the fire that marks an end to war
Ignite the world and end my lonely watch.

A single candle is lit at the altar in the southeast corner of the theater.

The Sentinel:
What is that light in the east? The flame
That signals a world-consuming fire,
The end of the city,
The end of Troy.

A spotlight illuminates the altar where the candle is burning, laying a thin line of light from northwest to southeast.

The Sentinel:
The King returns, Troy is no more,
At last the Queen rejoices,
Argos dances,
And I, I dance as well—
But I know too much to speak.
The story I must tell,
The beginning of the end
Of Troy, is the end
Of every city.

A cry of triumph from Clytemnestra, who appears at the altar and casts incense on the candle flame. A chorus of three old women gathers around the altar.

The Chorus:
God, whoever you may be, by whatever name addressed,
You decree that wisdom nails soul to
body, body to world with passion.
I surrender to necessity and tell the story
now, fixed in my solitude.

A light comes up on the stage, where the watcher still stands, now visible for the first time. As he watches the altar, a pregnant rabbit wanders onto the stage in front of him. Two huge birds of prey, one black, one white, swoop down from opposite corners at the back. They tear the rabbit apart, spattering blood, then attack one another. More blood. This image is mirrored on a large video or projection screen behind the watcher. The audience should experience this as a bloody scene from something like "Wild Kingdom."

The Chorus:
When Troy stood still, before the fire of war,
Before this fire that marks its end, before
The King avenged a mockery
Of his brother's hospitality, before
Our children were sacrificed
At the gates of Troy
To the inconstancy of Helen,
To the audacity of Paris,
The fleet lay in the harbor,

Stalled by contrary winds.
And, as the army watched entranced,
Two great birds of prey,
One white, one black,
Devoured a pregnant hare.
The seer Calchas read the act
As an affront to Artemis, a god,
Committed by god's emissaries,
And foresaw in the end of Troy
The end of Troy's destroyers,
A fatal contradiction at god's heart.
How, then, are we to address
A god who thus addresses us?

Agamemnon enters with his daughter, Iphigenia, who is bound and lifted over the altar.

The Chorus:
In the omen, Agamemnon saw himself,
his brother, and his daughter;
He saw necessity: a sacrifice to appease
Artemis, incensed at the slaughter.
To necessity he surrendered, and learned to read the stars,
Their rising and their setting fixed in his solitude.

Agamemnon slits her throat, and blood spurts out. The old women catch it in chalices while Clytemnestra watches in horror. Agamemnon disappears. Iphigenia's lifeless body remains draped over the altar.

The Chorus:
Iphigenia died first, a sacrifice before Troy, a sorrow
Song. Sorrow, sorrow, sing a sorrow song.
But in the end may good prevail.

They drink the blood and move into the audience, toward the altar at the northwest corner, offering the chalices.

The Chorus:
Take, drink. This is the blood of Iphigenia, shed for you.

The single candle on the altar flares into a raging flame, consuming Iphigenia's body. Lights come up behind the altar—dawn.

Clytemnestra:
To me this dawn is like a daughter,
Sacrificed before Troy, fallen,
Plundered by my King.

The chorus of old women, having finished distributing the blood of Iphigenia, return to the altar, each with a large (Paschal) candle. They light the candles from the fire and move into the audience, lighting the individual candles that were distributed to the audience at the beginning. The effect should be like an Easter vigil.

Clytemnestra:
The city that was music is now noise,
No harmony among its voices.
Vanquished voice distinct

From victor, as vinegar from oil,
Each fortune sings its own song.
Vanquished is a woman
Who mourns the death of every child
As the senseless death of her own.
Victor is a crowd of men,
Order disordered. Should they not
Offend the broken city's gods,
Honor her holy places,
They would be whole, not
Broken, home, not lost.
But it is too late already.
These gods are necessary
For accidental men making their way home.
Where death will break them still,
And the vanquished woman will sing
The death of every child
As the senseless death of her own,
A sorrow song. Sing,
Sing a sorrow song.
But in the end may good prevail.

The fire spreads.

Cassandra enters at the northeast altar, carrying a torch, followed by Agamemnon. Clytemnestra greets him. Clytemnestra kills Agamemnon at the northeast altar. Again, the chorus of old women catch the blood and distribute it to the audience. As with Iphigenia, the altar bursts into flame, consuming the body.

The Chorus (*repeating*):
Agamemnon died for your sins. This is
his blood, shed for you. Take, drink.

*The scene is repeated (more or less) with Cassandra at the
northwest altar.*

The Chorus (*repeating*):
Cassandra died for your sins. This is Cassandra's blood,
shed for you. Take, drink.

*Spotlight on Orestes (front, center). He offers a libation at his
father's grave, a Eucharistic prayer.*

Orestes:
God, god who guides souls and voices to the world below,
Carry my voice out of exile to my father.
With thanks, father, to the sacred river
That bore me in the place of my mother's absence,
I grieve that I was not present
In the moment of your death,
To mourn your passing,
To carry your corpse
To its place of rest.
God, grant me the grace of your assistance.
Grant me vengeance for my father's death.

*The chorus of old women approaches slowly from the back of
the theater, joined by Electra and the shade of Cassandra, all
dressed in mourning. Electra bears a thurible burning incense,
and the others carry offerings for a libation at Agamemnon's
tomb.*

Orestes:
But what is this?
A crowd of women
Winds its way here
Clothed in mourning—
Mourning for another sorrow
In the sorrow song this house sings?
No, Electra leads them,
First in sorrow:

It is mourning for my father
That brings them here with libations
To appease the powers below.

*Orestes moves into the shadows, invisible to the approaching
women, who move into the spotlight.*

The Chorus:
From the palace to the tomb I bear libation,
My whole life lamentation,
Torn by fortune that knows no joy,
Emissary of the Queen, shaken
This night from sleep
By the angry voice of a soul beneath the earth
Demanding justice of the one who sent him there.
She dispatched another graceless grace,
Not justice, but an offering to earth our mother.
What redemption is there for blood once fallen?
What libation can silence its cry and soothe the earth
Who sings the death of every child
As the senseless death of her own?

Electra (*to the whole Chorus, but particularly to Cassandra*):
Emissary of my mother's troubled sleep,
What song of sorrow shall I sing here at my father's tomb?
My own mother a loving wife who reaches
Through death's divide like Orpheus?
I do not hear that song. I do not
Hear it. Or shall I sing the common song,
Return the good of these funereal honors
To those who sing them—a gift

To match the evil that has brought us here?
Or shall I pour libation in silence,
Dishonored as my father was in death,
Retrace my steps, and fling the vessel
from me with averted eyes?

Cassandra:
At the altar of your father's tomb, I pray at your command.

Electra:
Speak as you honor my father's grave.

Cassandra:
As you pour, speak well of loyal hearts.

Electra:
And of those near me, who is worthy of that name?

Cassandra:
You first, and remember Orestes, far from home.
Sing in his memory. Do this in remembrance of him.

The Chorus:
Sing, sing a sorrow song. Sing for one
who shall take life for life.

Electra:
Life for life, in remembrance of him.
Forget my mother's troubled sleep.
God, god who guides souls and voices to the world below,
Carry my homeless voice out of exile to my father

In the place of my mother's absence.
God, grant me the grace of your assistance.
Grant me vengeance for my father's death.
Bring Orestes home,
With fortune that has not forgotten laughter.

Electra hands the thurible to Cassandra. The women of the chorus hand Electra the libation offerings. She pours the libation. Startled, she becomes aware of Orestes in the shadows, though she does not recognize him immediately.

Orestes (*stepping back into the light*):
God answers prayers. Pray now for success.

In the light, Electra recognizes Orestes. They embrace.

Electra:
O best beloved of our father's house,
With God's help may you bring us home
To the place of our mother's absence.
Beloved four times over,
I call you father in our father's absence;
The love due our mother—now hated as our father's killer;
The love I bore my sister, sacrificed; and
The love due my brother, our best hope—all fall to you.
God grant you the grace of his assistance.

Orestes:
If only our father had died before Troy,
Not at our mother's hand, the burden of our house
Would weigh less heavy.

But now, vengeance is God's.
Father, I call on you.
Rise up, and possess me with your anger.

Orestes turns to the chorus of old women.

Orestes:
Now, what drove my mother
To send you with these libations,
Too late to make requital
For an act beyond remedy?
What good are gifts to the dead?
To sacrifice everything in atonement
For fallen blood is labor lost.
What can you tell me?

The Chorus:
We are emissaries of the Queen's troubled sleep.
She dreamed she gave birth to a serpent,
And she wrapped it in swaddling clothes and laid it in a cradle.
When it was hungry, she gave it her own breast;
And with the milk of her breast, it drew blood.
She woke with a scream and sent us here
To offer libation for the restless dead.

Orestes:
I am the serpent.

The spotlight is cut, and the stage returns to darkness. Only the fires burning at the altars light the theater. When the light comes back up, Orestes confronts his mother, Clytemnestra,

front, center. She does not recognize him, and he pretends not
to recognize her.

Orestes:
I am a stranger.
Traveling here on business, I encountered a man,
A stranger to me as I to him,
who asked my way and told me his.
"Since you are bound for Argos," he said,
"carry a message for me
To the parents of Orestes. Tell them Orestes is dead."
If you will direct me to them, I will deliver the message.
They must hear it from me.

Clytemnestra (*grief-stricken*):
Your story is our end.
The curse that haunts this house
Reaches beyond my vision
Of a place of safety
And strips me one by one
Of all I love.

Orestes:
Forgive me the sorrow I have brought you.
Hospitality demanded that I honor the pledge
Made to that stranger on the road here.

Clytemnestra:
And hospitality demands that this house
Receive you with, as it would have without,

This news, which would have come here
With another stranger if not with you. You are welcome here.

Clytemnestra turns and speaks to an attendant.

Clytemnestra:
Prepare a room for the stranger, who is our guest.

Lights dim again. The theater is dark except for the fires on the altars, which, once lighted, burn to the end of the play. After a moment of silence, we hear a struggle and a death gasp. Cries for help from the direction of the struggle. Lights come up as a servant bursts into Clytemnestra's room, focused tightly on Clytemnestra and the servant.

Clytemnestra:
What is it? What is this cry for help
That rises through the whole house?

Servant:
The dead are killing the living.

Clytemnestra:
Oh God, I understand the riddle.
Give me a weapon. I have come to this.

The servant exits. The light expands to reveal Orestes, standing over a corpse. Now Clytemnestra recognizes him.

Clytemnestra:
Aegisthus, my love, dead.

Orestes:
You love this man?
Then you shall not abandon him in death.

Clytemnestra:
Stop, my child. Pity the breast that nourished you.
I gave you life, and with you I would grow old.

Orestes:
Murder my father, then make your home with me?

Clytemnestra:
Fate, my child, must share the blame.

Orestes:
Then it is fate that has decreed your death.

Clytemnestra:
This is the serpent to which I gave birth.

*Orestes kills Clytemnestra and drags the body through the au-
dience to the southwest altar. The chorus of old women, joined
by the shade of Cassandra, follow and collect the blood that
flows from her wound in chalices. Orestes lifts the body onto
the altar, which bursts into flame, consuming the remains
of Clytemnestra. The corpse of Aegisthus is left to rot in the
open. The chorus drinks the blood, then moves through the
audience, toward center front. They again offer the chalices.*

The Chorus:

This is Clytemnestra's blood, shed for you.

Take it. Drink it. Remember.

Spotlight on Orestes (front, center). He is surrounded by the Chorus of old women. Cassandra rises from the flames burning on the altar where she was sacrificed, no longer a shade. Clytemnestra, too, rises from the flames burning on the altar where she was sacrificed. Both join the Chorus, all

now playing the Furies who hound Orestes. Orestes is holding Clytemnestra's bloody robe.

The Chorus:
Remember. Remember Clytemnestra's blood, shed for you.

Clytemnestra:
This is the serpent to which I gave birth.

Orestes:
Fate must share the blame.

The Chorus:
And it is fate that has decreed our death.

Clytemnestra:
The city that was music is now noise,
No harmony among its voices.
Vanquished voice distinct
From victor, as vinegar from oil,
Each fortune sings its own song.
Vanquished is a woman
Who mourns the death of every child
As the senseless death of her own.
Victor is a crowd of men,
Order disordered. Should they not
Offend the broken city's gods,
Honor her holy places,
They would be whole, not
Broken, home, not lost.
But it is too late already.

These gods are necessary
For accidental men making their way home.
Where death will break them still,
And the vanquished woman will sing
The death of every child
As the senseless death of her own,
A sorrow song. Sing,
Sing a sorrow song.
But in the end may good prevail.

Orestes collapses. Clytemnestra and Cassandra hover over him.

The Chorus:
Iphigenia died first, a sacrifice before Troy, a sorrow
Song. Sorrow, sorrow, sing a sorrow song.
But in the end may good prevail.

The Furies move into the audience with chalices for a ritual eucharist that repeats the first.

The Chorus:
Take, drink. This is the blood of Iphigenia, shed for you.

Clytemnestra:
The dawn to me is like a daughter,
Sacrificed before Troy, fallen.

The stage where Orestes has collapsed begins to burn. Flames are raging now at each corner of the theater. In the end, the main stage goes up in flames as well, consuming the body of Orestes.

Chorus (chanting, while the fires rage):
A sorrow song. Sing, sing a sorrow song.

Fires burn themselves out. Darkness. Silence.

three: nirodha

15. Stop here, now, and all these deaths mean nothing.

be here now
would it be better that the
deaths _not_ mean nothing

what does it mean if the
deaths have no meaning?

Is die "bad"?

FOUR

Feed Your Life

My daughter Regina is a dealer in rare books who occasionally comes across a real treasure even when (perhaps especially when) she's not particularly expecting one. A few weeks ago, she was offered a first edition of Freud's *Der Witz und seine Beziehung zum Unbewussten*.

In excellent condition—and if it was really a first edition, it could be worth a pretty penny. But it had been stashed in a box in the attic with a bunch of papers and had been sitting there for twenty years with no climate control. The grandchildren of a collector came across it when they got around to cleaning the house before putting it on the market after their aunt, who had occupied the house for some years, died. None of them read German, but they recognized Freud, saw that the book was old, and thought it might be valuable. Just to be safe, they resisted the urge to throw out the papers, some of which appeared to be in German, others in a language they didn't recognize. One guessed Arabic, but none knew.

"It could be worse," she thought. "They could have kept it in the basement." So she went to have a look.

The book was well made, the attic dry and reasonably well ventilated—so Freud was in surprisingly good condition. The loose papers appeared to be notes taken while reading the book, German, in a tight, disciplined hand. Inside the box, there were two smaller boxes, each containing loose papers and scraps of papers. In one of these boxes, the papers, unbound but gathered with a string, were in Greek script as disciplined as the German. The other box was a mix of German and English notes, mostly references to other books—probably books that had been in the library but were now lost.

It wasn't possible to judge the value of the papers without closer examination. But the Freud was a find, so Regina offered them $500 for the box, which they readily accepted. She loaded it in the car and headed for home.

On closer examination, it was clear that mice had gotten into the box at some point. Although the papers had been rearranged, you could sort them by the extent of damage—from pieces that were pretty thoroughly shredded to those that had been untouched. There were bits of loose string still clinging to some of the papers. Regina surmised that whoever had packed the book away had put it between two stacks of notes, then bound the whole into one bundle. When the mice got in (and they must not have done so long before the exterminator was called), they shredded the papers on the outside. Those closer to the book, though, were in better shape; those closest were entirely undamaged. All those tightly disciplined and thoroughly pedestrian notes (not an original word or spark of creativity in the lot of them) had protected the book. So this first edition of Freud, in near perfect condition, was a little miracle of survival, an unexpected side effect of someone's neat fetish rather than a research project or even the outcome of a carefully considered strategy to protect a book while its value grew.

She separated the book from the remains of the notes and began to prepare it for shelving, planning to return later to the papers in the boxes in the box.

While carefully going through Freud page by page, inspecting for damage, she came across a scrap of old paper folded in half, tucked into the book, she guessed, to mark some reader's place. Unfolding it gently, she saw that it was in Greek—probably the same neat hand responsible for the German notes.

It was a poem—at least most of one—that began

Ποικιλόθρον' ἀθάνατ' Ἀφροδιτα,
παῖ Δίοσ, δολόπλοκε, λίσσομαί σε
μή μ' ἄσαισι μήτ' ὀνίαισι δάμνα,
πότνια, θῦμον.

Deathless Aphrodite of the rainbow throne,
child of Zeus, weaver of enchantment, I beg you
not to crush my soul with suffering and sorrow,
blessed queen.

At some point, it seems, the note-taker had transcribed a Greek text of Sappho—not such an unusual find, in that this particular bit of Sappho was known to have survived the burning of her collected works in Alexandria by zealous Christians and had been reproduced and translated many times. But, still, finding it tucked into Freud's *Witz* was, to say the least, serendipitous. And the two together added to the interest of the boxes in the box, especially the one that contained Greek.

Freud went on the shelf where he would be among old friends, periodically admired by people who wished they could afford such a book, who certainly thought it worth the price, but would not buy it.

And Regina went to work on the box of Greek fragments.

They fell into two groups.

One was a group of poems, some recognizably those of Sappho, familiar from translations, others not. It seems the note-taker had stumbled somewhere upon surviving fragments of Sappho otherwise unknown and transcribed them. They had apparently fallen into the hands of the collector—perhaps already bundled, perhaps bundled later, by the collector or the meticulous packer who'd put this box together before it was stashed in the attic.

The other appeared to be a fragment of dialogue—a scene from a play, perhaps, or part of one, translated here in the style of a short story to make it easier to follow.

It begins in the middle:

That, essentially, is what Phaedrus said, as it was reported to me by Aristodemus. Several speeches followed, he said, that he could not remember clearly (and one he wished he could forget). So he was ready to proceed directly to the speech of Pausanius, passing over the others.

Of course, my friend was as curious as either of us, so he immediately said he didn't much care about Pausanius right now but would really love to hear the speech his friend wanted to forget. In the first place, if he wanted to forget it, it stands to reason that he remembered it—probably better than all the others. And, in the second place, whatever made him want to forget it probably meant that it contained something worth remembering (that is, something good enough to make you think you should forget).

So my friend pressed Aristodemus, who said "It wasn't really a speech—more of a curious outburst that threatened to disrupt the whole conversation. That's why I usually don't tell it (or even mention it) when I recount the story."

I'm certain you agree, Glaucon, that a symposium of reasonable men distracted by an unplanned outburst could hardly be called a rational undertaking. Such an outburst would undermine the whole affair.

"All the more reason to tell it, Apollodorus, because its entertainment value is sure to wax as its rationality wanes."

Exactly what I said, Glaucon. But my friend said, "Really, Apollodorus, It was the emotional outburst of a woman, no more worth remembering than a sudden thunderstorm."

"A woman? Then I must hear it. How on earth would a woman find her way into a gathering like the one you have begun to describe? What would Socrates say about such a thing?"

If you insist. But, really, as my friend said, it just makes the story longer and delays hearing what Socrates had to say about love.

"Yes. Absolutely. I insist. Socrates can wait."

Very well. This is how Aristodemus told the story when *I* insisted.

You remember the *aulos* player that the party sent away. Agathon told her to entertain herself or play for the women of the house. She left the room where the party was gathered, but it seems she didn't go far. As it turned out, she was one of those girls with too much education for her own good. Her idea of entertainment included sitting just outside the door where she could hear the speeches. In fact, she found that far more enjoyable than the drunken banter she usually had to endure when she was called on to perform for such a party. So she tucked the *aulos* into her skirt and sat against the wall where she could hear.

At first, she was less interested in the speeches than in the murmuring conversation of the servants who (you will recall) had been instructed to act as though they themselves were giving the party. The servants were keeping themselves amused by arguing quietly over who should be considered the chief guest. For some, it was Socrates, without question. Others thought Agathon, especially since he was like a playwright who had cast them as host. A few thought Aristodemus, because his unexpected entrance made him the center of attention before Socrates arrived.

But when Phaedrus began talking about how no one had sung proper hymns to love, she gave him her full attention.

She knew the stories about Aphrodite well, because she had spent time in a gymnasium founded by a disciple of Sappho. There she received such thorough training in music and poetry that she became particularly successful as a performer, a master of *aulos*. But she knew the stories well, so she knew love was no god, and she knew that it was passion that made Aphrodite as powerful in her own way as Ares.

As Phaedrus was concluding, with his comment about Love as the most ancient of the gods, how he was the most powerful in helping men gain virtue, the party heard the unmistakable sound of the *aulos*.

Agathon rose and stepped out into the hall, where he found the girl playing.

"I told you to go entertain yourself or play for the women of the house."

She stopped then and did the most remarkable thing. She looked Agathon directly in the eye and said, "I am."

"You are *what*?" he said.

"I am entertaining myself and playing for the women of the house."

"You are disrupting our conversation. Go play somewhere else."

"But that would be neither entertaining myself nor playing for the women—and so it would be disobeying your command."

Agathon would have struck her if Socrates had not stepped in. "Let her speak," he said. "Wisdom is full of surprises, so why shouldn't she speak in a young girl's voice?"

She laughed.

Agathon was so astonished that he did not strike her. The whole group was struck dumb, and she began to sing. It was something Sappho had written, something about Aphrodite. (Aristophanes was so shocked by this whole turn of events that he began to hiccup, which detracted somewhat from the performance. Fortunately, the girl had a strong voice, and the power of it restrained even Aristophanes. He held back for the time being.)

And she sang.

῎Εστι μοι κάλα πάισ χρυσίοισιν ἀνθέμοισιν
ἐμφέρην ἔχοισα μόρφαν, Κλῆισ ἀγαπάτα,
ἀντι τᾶσ ἔγω οὐδὲ Λυδίαν παῖσαν οὐδ' ἔρανναν.
My daughter is to me as beautiful as
sparkling flowers of gold, Kleis,
loved more than Lydia, more than lovely Lesbos.

In the end, silence.

Then the guest who was to speak after Phaedrus said, "Teach me to sing that song."

Agathon, recovered enough to be angry again, said "Why on earth would you ask her to be your teacher?"

"So I can die," replied the guest.

At that, Agathon shooed the girl away and she left, followed by three of the guests.

The others reassembled without a word and went directly to the speech of Pausanius.

four: yang sheng

16. To connect knowledge with desire (as Diotima does in her contribution to the *Symposium*) is to offer a rudimentary theory of motivation within the context of epistemology. It responds to the fundamental question *what drives our knowing*? Note that in the story we have a story teller, a listener, at least three writers, a collector, a compulsive note-taker, a packer with a neat fetish, an unspecified number of mice, a buyer of old books, a tragic poet, a comic poet, one or more philosophers (all in a dialogue that, here, goes without saying), and two or more bodies of readers that may overlap and may continue to grow—all in some sense acting in ways that contribute to knowledge, all brought into the circle of our awareness by virtue of their desire and ours.

17. This rudimentary theory leaves the specification of desire and knowledge to the imagination. Both are without content, empty words ready to serve our organizational ends.

18. But Plato, like Freud, connects *desire* with the physical and uses Diotima (through Socrates) to claim that *physical* desire (particularly sexual desire, *eros*) is the fuel on which knowing (a process of possession rather than an object to be possessed) runs.

Desire, object-oriented, aims for possession—what Hans Furth, in his essay on Piaget and Freud, called "want my object." For Furth as for Diotima, the structure of desire remains constant throughout human development, but there is a shift in the construction of the object generally understood as a movement from concrete to formal. This is the Piagetian distinction articulated by Furth between action knowledge and object knowledge—which we might also characterize as a transition from present/concrete to possible/abstract.

19. To the extent that Plato (or Plato's Socrates) is understood as "rising above" physical desire to a state of detachment, pure knowledge might be identified simply with logic (which is how Piaget has sometimes been understood).

20. The result would be to extract knowledge from the world of bodies (where we live) and locate it in a world of no bodies (where we do not). Pure knowledge requires a knower, but this knower would be no body. Platonic love, then, would be disembodied, lifeless love.

21. But Plato's Socrates suggests that the separation is a dangerous distortion. In the *Symposium*, from beginning to end, he is engaged in an ordinary practice that includes philosophical argument, drinking with his friends, the care of the body. He does not rise above the ordinary into some extraordinary realm and return to it: he never leaves it. (Piagetian theory, too, in the transition from present/concrete

to possible/abstract, remains embodied. It is an expansion of desire from "want my object" into a field where one may imagine oneself as an object among objects—and, when formal operations become fully reversible, take the perspective of the constructed object, which then becomes the constructing subject. This is not a matter of stepping outside oneself but rather of reconfiguring self to include the possibility of other perspectives, other selves. This may be understood   as a contribution to the construction of a social self, a body politic.)

22.   The *Symposium*, as a dialogue of uninvited guests and improvised hosts, poses a central question for epistemology in the form of a moral discourse: confronted with what doesn't fit, what do we do? (Or, to put it another way, how do we welcome strangers into our midst?) We act in such a way as to make it fit—either by incorporating it or adapting to it. (We change it or we change ourselves.) In our interaction with the environment, there is a rhythm of incorporation and adaptation. (In Piaget, "our" is not limited to the human, and the rhythm is a process of equilibration.)

23.   A logic of the concrete (Bergson's geometry of solids) is at work in our work on the world (and its work on us). We are driven not entirely by desire for wholeness (though Aristophanes has a point) or harmony (though Eryximachus does as well) but by the *necessity* of place. As embodied beings, we *must*

take place—so too the embodied beings (things, objects, persons) we encounter.

24.   To take place and give place, we make place in the process of constructing structures that contain the new—but never entirely, because we are embodied beings in finite space. Cognitively, the challenge is to make sense. Physically, the challenge is to make room. Politically, the challenge is to make a city. There is room at the table for Aristodemus, for Alcibiades and the drunken revelers. Socrates makes room for the *aulos* player when she, playing, takes place. (Though as the dialogue comes to us from Plato, the *aulos* player and Diotima are present by their absence when Socrates speaks.) That, in the end, is why he can drink comedy and tragedy under the table without once stepping outside his life.

25.   Plato's dialogue is a moral discourse because it is *about* Socrates, who is the exemplar of virtue. The dialogue takes place about Socrates, about a person, in that it dances and plays around him. Its form is the form of a conversation in which an embodied person is the nucleus. In the missing speech, the dialogue is about the *aulos* player, and that, too, is a moral discourse, for which the fundamental question is how to include the uninvited guest at the table—especially if including the uninvited guest at the table requires that the table itself be fundamentally changed. The *aulos* player plays to call attention to something the others do not know or know and do not say. The guests that follow the *aulos*

player remind us that desire is doubly object oriented—aiming both to possess and to be possessed. The guest who asks to learn the song so he can die gestures toward the perfection of the song (which is why music has so often served as a metaphor for humanity: we *are* the music, as Virginia Woolf said) but also reminds us of our living toward dying. Desire is doubly object oriented, and it informs our living toward death and toward the other, both of which always ensure something other to be encountered and encountered by, both of which ensure that there may always be a stranger at the door, always a new song, always a city that is therefore always new.

Sources

A NOTE TO THE READER

The pieces gathered in this collection have evolved over several decades, aided and abetted by a number of key sources and conversations.

The first version of the first chapter, "Job's Cat," was triggered by a close reading of Job with students and colleagues at Capital University in Ohio. Another group of students and colleagues at Roosevelt University in Chicago who joined me in a reading of Stephen Mitchell's translation of Job further shaped the story. Long before the short story itself was written, Richard Luecke introduced me to George Dennis O'Brien's "Prolegomena to a Dissolution to the Problem of Suffering" and Søren Kierkegaard's reading of Job (in the voice of Constantin Constantius) in *Repetition*. Leibniz's *Theodicy* and Archibald Macleish's *J.B.* have also contributed to my thinking on this subject.

The first version of the second chapter, "Why Sarah Laughed," began with conversations on the theme of "sacrifice" in humanities classes at Calumet College of St. Joseph, the University of Northern Iowa, and Roosevelt University. The primary sources are Genesis 22, Judges 11, and Qur'an 37. Kierkegaard's reading of the Abraham story in *Fear and Trembling* and Jacques Derrida's reading of that reading in

The Gift of Death have been particularly influential on my tellings of the tale, as has Phyllis Trible's *Texts of Terror*. Long conversations with Yang Qian and Mary Ann O'Donnell in Chicago and Shenzhen have further shaped my tellings, as has Stanley Hauerwas's meditation on the seven last words of Jesus in *Cross-Shattered Christ*.

The third chapter, "Oresteia: A Homecoming," also began in conversations in classes at Roosevelt University and was further shaped by conversation with students in the Basic Program of Liberal Education for Adults at the University of Chicago. Ted Hughes's beautiful translation has been particularly important to my reading of the plays.

The fourth chapter, "Feed Your Life," began with a seminar on Plato's Symposium in the Basic Program. It was further shaped by conversations with colleagues at Shenzhen University, particularly Zhao Dongming, and by close reading of Sappho's fragments (some translations of which found their way into the text). The reflections at the end of this chapter draw especially on François Jullien's *Vital Nourishment: Departing from Happiness* and Hans Furth's *Knowledge as Desire: an Essay on Freud and Piaget*.

Influencing my thinking throughout is a running conversation with my daughter Regina that has now entered its fourth decade and a conversation with my friend and colleague Sou Vai Keng that began on the street in Macao, turned into a series of collaborations in poetry and painting, and continues through her paintings in response to this book.

Aeschylus. *The Oresteia*. Translated by Ted Hughes. New York: Farrar, Straus, and Giroux, 2000.

Derrida, Jacques. *The Gift of Death*. Translated by David Wills. Chicago: University of Chicago Press, 1996.

Furth, Hans G. *Knowledge as Desire: An Essay on Freud and Piaget*. New York: Columbia University Press, 1990.

Hauerwas, Stanley. *Cross-Shattered Christ: Meditations on the Seven Last Words*. Grand Rapids, Michigan: Brazos Press, 2005.

Jullien, François. *Vital Nourishment: Departing from Happiness*. Cambridge, Massachusetts: Zone Books, 2007.

Kierkegaard, Søren. *Fear and Trembling / Repetition*. Edited and Translated by Howard V. Hong and Edna H. Hong. Princeton, New Jersey: Princeton University Press, 1983.

Leibniz, Gottfried Wilhelm. *Theodicy*. Translated by E. M. Huggard. New York: Cosimo, 2009.

MacLeish, Archibald. *J.B.: A Play in Verse*. New York: Houghton Mifflin, 1989.

O'Brien, George Dennis. "Prolegomena to a Dissolution to the Problem of Suffering." *Harvard Theological Review* 57:4 (Oct., 1964), 301-23.

The Book of Job. Translated by Stephen Mitchell. New York: HarperCollins, 1992.

Trible, Phyllis. *Texts of Terror: Literary-Feminist Readings of Biblical Narratives*. Minneapolis: Fortress Press, 1984.